WEIRD BUT TRUE SCIENCE

Weird But True Food

Series Science Consultant:
Mary Poulson, PhD
Central Washington University
Ellensburg, WA

Series Literacy Consultant:
Allan A. De Fina, PhD
Dean, College of Education/Professor of Literacy Education
New Jersey City University
Past President of the New Jersey Reading Association

Carmen Bredeson

CONTENTS

WORDS TO KNOW

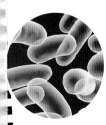 **bacteria** **[bak TEER ee uh]**—Very tiny living things that you can only see with a microscope. Bacteria can be found in all living things.

 **carrageenan [kar uh GEE nihn]**—A type of seaweed. When it is boiled, it makes a thick juice that is used in some foods.

 **digest [dy JEST]**—To change food into smaller parts that can be used by the body.

 **protein** **[PROH teen]**—Food such as meat, fish, beans, eggs, and milk.

The food pyramid shows you what types
of food to eat every day.

MyPyramid For Kids
Eat Right. Exercise Have Fun.
MyPyramid.gov

Grains
Make half your grains whole

Vegetables
Vary your veggies

Fruits
Focus on fruits

Milk
Get your calcium-rich foods

Meat & Beans
Go lean with protein

Oils   Oils are not a food group, but you need some for good health. Get your oils from fish, nuts, and liquid oils such as corn oil, soybean oil, and canola oil.

★ Find your balance between food and fun   ★ Fats and sugars — know your limits

MyPyramid.gov
STEPS TO A HEALTHIER YOU

WEIRD FOOD

Our bodies need food to grow and to be healthy.
We all know that fruits and vegetables are good to eat.
But what about crickets and seaweed? How would you
like to eat them for lunch with a big glass of cow blood?

Let's read about some weird—but true—food!

Pizza

Want a little fish with that pie?

What is your favorite pizza topping? How about eel or squid? Both of these are common toppings in Japan. In Brazil, some pizzas are served with green peas and boiled eggs on top. YUM!

It's weird, but it's true!

Pizza is a grain, vegetable, and protein.
This pizza has small fish on it!

Durian is a fruit.

Durian

Hold your nose!

Have you ever seen a fruit as big as a soccer ball? A durian [DOOR ee uhn] fruit is huge! The inside is filled with a creamy custard. But there is one BIG problem. This fruit smells like dead fish or dirty toilets! Hold your nose while you eat it!

It's weird, but it's true!

SWISS CHEESE

How did the holes get there?

Cheese is made with milk. **Bacteria** are added.
The bacteria start to eat and **digest** the milk.
Then the bacteria let off gas, kind of like burps.
The gas bubbles get trapped in the milk.
The bubbles leave holes in the cheese.

It's weird, but it's true!

Cheese is milk, protein, and fat.

Rose petals are a vegetable.

ROSE PETALS

Can I sniff your soup?

Roses smell sweet. They taste sweet, too.
But who eats roses? A lot of people!
The petals are used in soups, salads, and ice cream.
They add beautiful colors to food. Sniff. Sniff.

It's weird, but it's true!

CARRAGEENAN

There's seaweed in the ice cream!

Look at a carton of ice cream. Read the list of things that were used to make it. Is **carrageenan** on the list? It is a kind of SEAWEED! It makes a thick, jelly-like juice when boiled. The juice is added to ice cream and other foods to make them thicker.

It's weird, but it's true!

This woman collects seaweed.
It will be used to make carrageenan.

fruit

Prickly pear flowers turn into fruit.

Prickly Pear Cactus

Don't stab your tongue!

American Indians ate a lot of prickly pear cactus. The fruit is sweet and tasty. Other parts of the cactus can be made into flour. People today still eat prickly pear. Be sure to cut off the thorns first! Ouch.

It's weird, but it's true!

FRIED CRICKETS
Would you like catsup with that?

We eat baskets of french fries in the United States. In Vietnam, you can order a basket of fried crickets with dipping sauce. They come with the heads and legs attached! What a CRUNCHY treat!

It's weird, but it's true!

Fried crickets are protein and fat.

BLOOD

Cheers!

In parts of Africa, there is not much meat to eat. People drink cow blood to get **protein**. They cut the vein of a cow. The cow's blood drips into a bowl. When the bowl is full, they drink the blood. SLURP!

It's weird, but it's true!

Cow's blood is protein.

LEARN MORE

Books

Kleinberg, Naomi. *Grover's Guide to Good Eating*. NY: Random House, 2007.

Schaefer, A. R. *Healthy Food*. Chicago: Heinemann Library, 2010.

Taylor-Butler, Christine. *The Food Pyramid*. New York: Children's Press, 2008.

LEARN MORE

Web Sites

Nemours. Explore the Food Guide Pyramid

http://www.kidshealth.org/kids/stay_healthy/food/fgp_
  interactive.html

USDA. My Pyramid for Kids

http://www.fns.usda.gov/tn/resources/mpk_poster.pdf

INDEX

To our wonderful grandchildren: Andrew, Charlie, Kate, and Caroline

Enslow Elementary, an imprint of Enslow Publishers, Inc.

Enslow Elementary® is a registered trademark of Enslow Publishers, Inc.

Library of Congress Cataloging-in-Publication Data

Bredeson, Carmen.
  Weird but true food / Carmen Bredeson.
    p. cm. — (Weird but true science)
  Includes index.
  Summary: "Read about some unusual foods like durian, prickly pear cactus, fried crickets, and others"—Provided by publisher.
  ISBN 978-0-7660-3866-0
  1. Food—Miscellanea—Juvenile literature. I. Title.
  TX355.B745 2011
  641.3 dc22
                        2010035860

Paperback ISBN: 978-1-59845-367-6

Printed in China

052011 Leo Paper Group, Heshan City, Guangdong, China

10 9 8 7 6 5 4 3 2 1

To Our Readers: We have done our best to make sure all Internet Addresses in this book were active and appropriate when we went to press. However, the author and the publisher have no control over and assume no liability for the material available on those Internet sites or on other Web sites they may link to. Any comments or suggestions can be sent by e-mail to comments@enslow.com or to the address on the back cover.

Photo Credits: Alamy: © Philip Game, pp. 3 (woman), 15, © Rebecca Marsden, p. 19; © iStockphoto.com/Miha Krivic, p. 3 (protein); © John Warburton-Lee Photography/Photolibrary, p. 21; © Photos.com, p. 3 (hamburger); Shutterstock.com, pp. 2, 3 (bacteria), 8, 11, 12, 13, 14, 16; © Thelma & Louise/StockFood, pp. 1, 7; U.S. Department of Agriculture, p. 4.

Cover Photo: © Thelma & Louise/StockFood

Note to Parents and Teachers: The *Weird But True Science* series supports the National Science Education Standards for K–4 science. The Words to Know section introduces subject-specific vocabulary words, including pronunciation and definitions. Early readers may need help with these new words.

Enslow Elementary
an imprint of
Enslow Publishers, Inc.
40 Industrial Road
Box 398
Berkeley Heights, NJ 07922
USA
http://www.enslow.com